PEPYS AND THE STUARTS

Stewart Ross

Illustrated by Gerry Wood

Wayland

LIFE AND TIMES

Alexander the Great and the Greeks
Julius Caesar and the Romans
Alfred the Great and the Saxons
Canute and the Vikings
William the Conqueror and the Normans
Richard the Lionheart and the Crusades
Columbus and the Age of Exploration
Montezuma and the Aztecs
Elizabeth I and Tudor England
Oliver Cromwell and the Civil War
Pepys and the Stuarts
Daniel Boone and the American West

Further titles are in preparation

First published in 1985 by
Wayland (Publishers) Ltd
49 Lansdowne Place, Hove
East Sussex BN3 1HF, England

ISBN 0 85078 575 8

Phototypeset by Planagraphic Typesetters Ltd
Printed in Italy by G. Canale & C.S.p.A., Turin
Bound in the U.K. by The Bath Press

Contents

1 **THE STORY OF SAMUEL PEPYS**
The man who kept a diary 4
The young Londoner 6
The civil servant 8

2 **THE HOUSE OF STUART**
James I: the first Stuart 10
Charles I and the Civil War 12
Charles II and the Restoration 14
James II 16
William and Mary: the 1688 Revolution 18
Anne, and Marlborough's wars 20

3 **THE CHANGING YEARS**
Monarch and Parliament 22
Industry and trade 24
Anglicans and Puritans 26
Roman Catholics 28

4 **STUART LONDON**
Pepys's city 30
The court and courtiers 32
Taverns and coffee-houses 34
In the backstreets 36
Plague and fire 38
Arts and architecture 40

5 **COUNTRY TOWNS**
Bristol — a thriving port 42
Oxford — a royal town 44

6 **COUNTRY LIFE**
On the farm 46
In the village 48
Sports and pastimes 50
Crime and punishment 52

7 **THE STUART AGE 55**

Table of dates 56
Glossary 57
Further information 58
Index 59

Above *Samuel Pepys (1633-1703).*

1 THE STORY OF SAMUEL PEPYS

The man who kept a diary

London. 10 September 1663. It is early evening. A young man sits at his desk by an open first-floor window. He dips his quill pen into the ink, and writes in his diary:

'Got up and went to the office. Spent all the morning making a contract with Sir William Warren. I am buying £3,000 worth of masts for the navy's ships. But, good God, what a profit I could make for myself if I were a crook!'

This evening he is writing about his work, but sometimes he writes very personal details about his wife and friends. They would never forgive him if they could see some of the things he has written about them. So his diary is written in code, and he keeps it hidden.

The man writing the diary was Samuel Pepys. His diaries were private, but more than one hundred years after his death they were translated and published. The diaries of Samuel Pepys, kept between 1660 and 1669, now tell us more than anything else about life in seventeenth century England.

Pepys lived at a most exciting time. He witnessed plague, fire and several wars. Britain was ruled by a fascinating royal family, the Stuarts. One or two were excellent politicians, others were hopeless. One king had his head cut off, another fled from the country because he was so unpopular. Nevertheless, by the time Pepys died in 1703, the country was settling down, and the modern system of government had been born.

Opposite *Samuel Pepys started his famous diaries in 1660, the year that Charles II was restored to the English throne. He kept a diary for nine years and they tell us about life in Stuart England.*

The young Londoner

Above *A medal of Charles I, King of England from 1625-49.*

Samuel Pepys was born in London on 23 February 1633. His father was a tailor and his mother a washmaid. They lived in a fairly comfortable house in Fleet Street. Mrs Pepys had eleven children, of which Samuel was the fifth. Sadly, his four older brothers and sisters soon died, leaving Samuel the oldest child.

When he was thirteen, Samuel was sent to the famous St. Paul's School in London. Civil war raged in the 1640s and the streets were often full of soldiers. In 1649 Samuel even saw King Charles I having his head cut off.

Samuel Pepys was popular at school, and the masters liked him because he was intelligent. He had won a

scholarship to St. Paul's, and then one to Magdalen College, Cambridge in 1651. At this time he supported Oliver Cromwell and the Roundheads — in later life he was afraid that his school friends would remember this, and tell the authorities.

In 1654 Pepys took his first job, as secretary to the leading politician, Sir Edward Montague. The next year he married Elizabeth St. Michael. In his diary in 1666 he wrote that Elizabeth still made him 'happier and happier every day'.

1660 was an important year for Samuel Pepys. He started his diary. He also went to Holland to escort King Charles II back from exile to England, arriving at Dover, on 26 May (see page 14). When Pepys talked to the king he wrote in his diary that Charles 'made me ready to weep to hear . . . of his difficulties'.

Below *The young Pepys witnessed the execution of Charles I at Whitehall in 1649. The king was beheaded because the victorious Roundheads blamed him for all the deaths during the Civil War (1642-49).*

The civil servant

The grateful Charles II appointed Pepys clerk to the Navy Board. The king had almost no army. He relied upon 156 excellent ships to protect his kingdom. The Navy Board was responsible for keeping these ships in good fighting order.

Pepys worked hard, but he lived in difficult times. In 1665 and 1666 plague and fire swept through London (see page 38). To make matters worse, in 1667 the Dutch navy sailed up the River Medway in Kent, and destroyed many English ships. The navy was disgraced, and Pepys was so worried that he 'hardly slept all night'.

At the end of May 1669 Pepys stopped writing his diary. Later that year Elizabeth Pepys died. He was heartbroken. Despite his unhappiness, his career flourished.

Pepys became Secretary to the Admiralty and a Member of Parliament in 1673. Later he was unfairly accused of treason, and spent several weeks in the Tower of London. When James II came to the throne in 1685 his luck changed when the king employed him as Secretary for Naval Affairs. Pepys now knew more about the navy than anyone else, and James II trusted him a great deal.

Bad luck returned in 1688. James II was driven out of the country, and all his old servants were under suspicion. Pepys went to prison again. This was too much for him, and he decided to retire. He spent the remaining years of his life as a scholar. When he died in 1703 he left a wonderful library of 3,000 books. Six of these were his secret diaries.

Below *One of the jobs Pepys did when he was Secretary to the Admiralty was to ensure that sea-going ships were well-stocked with supplies.*

Above *James I, King of England from 1603-25.*

2 THE HOUSE OF STUART

James I: The first Stuart

Samuel Pepys was not alive during the reign of the first king from the House of Stuart. James I was a foreigner in England. He was born in Scotland in 1566, the son of Mary, Queen of Scots, and he had been king of that nation since 1567. In those days England and Scotland were completely different countries. They had separate religions, laws, customs and governments. So when James became King of England in 1603, Englishmen were suspicious of him and his Scottish friends.

Luckily James was an intelligent man, who had plenty of experience in government. As king of Scotland he had brought order to one of the most undisciplined nations in Europe. The new king did have faults, however. He was lazy and extravagant; he had favourites, and was too fond of the sound of his own voice.

England was not an easy country to govern. The king was always short of money. He had no police force or army, so he had to rely on powerful families to help him with the government. Parliament could be awkward too,

Opposite *During James I's journey from Scotland to claim the English throne in 1603 he was met by a group of churchmen who presented him with a petition begging him to be tolerant in religious affairs.*

especially when the government asked for money.

Despite the problems, at first James's reign went well. He ended England's war with Spain. He carefully avoided annoying the two difficult religious groups, the Catholics and the Puritans. His court was lively and glamorous. Some courtiers felt that they were in a new golden age.

By 1625, the year the king died, the mood had changed. Government debts had risen to £1 million, and England was at war again. James had failed to reward all the powerful groups of courtiers. The king's favourites, chosen for their good looks and not their brains, seemed to get all the money and all the good jobs.

Charles I and the Civil War

Above *A portrait of Charles I.*

Charles I — James's son — was a small, delicate man with a stammer. He loved collecting beautiful things, and he was devoted to his family. But he was not suited to being a king. He was aloof, unreliable and tactless.

The first five years of Charles's reign were difficult. The king's favourite, the Duke of Buckingham, had involved the country in wars with France and Spain, which the government could not afford. Parliament disliked Buckingham, and did not help to raise taxes to pay for the army and navy.

Buckingham was assassinated in 1628. The next year Charles decided to make peace, and rule without Parliament. Although he was short of money, for a while his plan went well. Then the king and his Archbishop of Canterbury, William Laud, foolishly tried to make the

religion of Scotland more like that of England. The Scots rebelled and invaded England.

Charles was forced to call Parliament again. For two years the king squabbled with Members of Parliament about the way the country should be governed. In the autumn of 1642, two sides formed and civil war broke out. Most Englishmen tried not to get involved.

The fighting and arguing went on for seven more years. The king was defeated many times, but he would not stick to any agreement with Parliament. By late 1648 Charles's enemies had had enough: on 30 January 1649 they executed the king. It looked as if there would be no more Stuarts on the throne of England.

Above *A woodcut published at the start of the Civil War (1642) shows how people at the time thought the world had gone crazy.*

Below *During the battle of Naseby in 1645 Charles tried to regroup his cavalry for an attack on the Roundheads. But it was too late. The battle was already lost, and his last real chance of winning the Civil War had gone.*

Above *Dutch ships raided Chatham docks in 1667 causing great damage to English shipping.*

Charles II and the Restoration

Above *Charles II, King of England from 1660-85.*

After the execution of Charles I England was without a king for eleven years. But Oliver Cromwell, who governed England for much of this time, found that he had many of the same problems as his old enemy, Charles I. So in 1660, two years after Cromwell's death, Charles I's son was invited back to England. Pepys, as we have seen, was a member of the party sent to collect him from Holland.

Charles II was not like his father. He was lazy. He wasn't very serious-minded either. He spent much time at the races, or pursuing the pretty ladies of the court. But he was highly intelligent. Above all, he was determined never to be driven off the throne.

At this time France was the most powerful country in

Europe. The French king, Louis XIV, threatened to overwhelm smaller states, such as England and Holland. His armies seemed unstoppable. The French were also Catholic. Ever since the time of Elizabeth I (1558-1603) most Englishmen hated Catholics: they saw them as their bitterest enemies.

Charles II and his Portuguese wife Catherine had no children. The person due to become king when Charles died was his brother, James. But James was a Catholic, and this made him very unpopular.

For a time, between 1679 and 1681, it looked as if there might be another civil war in England, between those who supported James and those who opposed him. With brilliant skill Charles II avoided war. When he died in 1685 the Stuarts were as safely on the throne as they had ever been.

Below *Charles II made a victorious procession through the streets of London to celebrate his restoration to the English throne in 1660.*

James II

Above *James Scott, the Duke of Monmouth, was executed in 1685 after a rebellion aimed at making him king had failed.*

Like his father, James II was no politician. He was a pleasant man, and quite able in military matters: Pepys was his special Secretary for Naval Affairs, and helped him a great deal. But James did not understand people. He was a Roman Catholic, and he could not see why Catholics were so unpopular in England. He tried to change people's attitudes, and he failed.

In 1688 James faced a rebellion led by James Scott, Duke of Monmouth. He was the illegitimate son of Charles II and thought by some to be the true king. At the battle of Sedgemoor Monmouth was defeated by James II's troops. Later he was executed and his supporters were cruelly punished.

James then went ahead with his policy of helping the Catholics. He swept aside anti-Catholic laws and said that they could worship as they wished. He built up a large army, with some Catholic officers.

James's behaviour was of great concern to the Protestant lords. News that the queen had given birth to a son, which meant that there was a Catholic heir to the throne, had great effect. Many nobles had already been in contact with the Protestant ruler of Holland, William of Orange — who was married to James's daughter Mary — and on June 30, 1688 they sent him a letter inviting him to bring an army to England to overthrow the king.

William landed in England on 6 November 1688. Men flocked to him. James's army melted away, and in December the unfortunate king fled to France. He never returned to England.

Above *James II, King of England from 1685-88.*

Opposite *James II, while fleeing from the country in 1688, dropped the Great Seal (a royal stamp of authority on acts of government) into the River Thames. He mistakenly believed that there could be no real government without it.*

Above *Although no blood was shed in England, there were Jacobite rebellions in Scotland and Ireland. The townspeople of Londonderry, who were loyal to William and Mary, starved while they withstood a long siege by Jacobite troops.*

William and Mary: The 1688 Revolution

Above *A medal of William and Mary.*

William III was not popular in England. He was an unsmiling foreigner, who was much more interested in Holland than in England. The reasons that he had been made king were because he was a Protestant, and because he was married to James II's daughter.

Mary was liked better than William because she was friendly and kind. But she never settled down in England, and she never forgot that she was queen in place of her father. This made her feel guilty for what she had done.

The powerful families of England were determined that no king should ever again behave like James II. Parliament

passed a Bill of Rights. This set limits on the king's power. For example, he couldn't have an army unless Parliament agreed. They also limited the amount of money the king received. The removal of James II, and the arrangements that followed, were called the Glorious Revolution. People called it glorious because no king could ever be a tyrant again.

James and his supporters (known as Jacobites) didn't accept the Revolution without a fight. There were wars in both Scotland and Ireland, but in the end they were defeated. James finally retired to his court at St. Germain, in France.

Mary died in 1694. William lived for another eight years, but he had a troubled time. An expensive war dragged on against France, while the political parties, Whigs and Tories, squabbled bitterly in Parliament. The exhausted king finally died after a riding accident in 1702.

Above *James Stuart, the son of James II, whose supporters — the Jacobites — believed he was the true heir to the throne after his father's death in 1701.*

Above *Anne, Queen of England from 1702-14.*

Above *John Churchill, 1st Duke of Marlborough, a brilliant general who won four famous military victories against the French.*

Anne, and Marlborough's wars

Queen Anne was the second daughter of James II and was married to George of Denmark. Although the couple had sixteen children, not one of them lived for long. So when Anne died in 1714 the Stuart line came to an end.

Anne was a worthy queen. She was a little serious, and rather overweight. Her court was never jolly, and lady favourites influenced her a great deal. Nevertheless, she chose her ministers wisely and England was sensibly governed throughout her reign.

Early in her reign, Anne's great favourite and friend was Sarah Churchill. Sarah was the wife of a leading Whig politician, John Churchill. For a time, therefore, the Whigs were in power.

The Whigs were worried in case Louis XIV should gain control of Spain. Under the leadership of Churchill and Sidney Godolphin, England joined with Holland, Austria and other European countries to fight France.

John Churchill was a brilliant general. In four great battles (Blenheim, Ramillies, Oudenarde and Malplaquet) he defeated the French. France itself was invaded. Then Sarah Churchill fell out with Queen Anne and the Whigs lost power. John Churchill (who had been made Duke of Marlborough) was dismissed, and the Tories made peace.

By the time Anne died England and Scotland had been joined as one country (1707). The throne of both countries now passed to a distant Protestant German relation, who became King George I. For her liberty and prosperity, Britain was now the envy of Europe.

Opposite *In 1701 several European countries formed an alliance against France which had become very powerful under its king, Louis XIV. Queen Anne discussed how the war against France should be fought with her closest advisers, Sarah and John Churchill.*

Above *Elections for Parliament were rowdy occasions in which only a few people were allowed to vote.*

3 THE CHANGING YEARS

Above *Sick people came to the court of Charles II in the hope that they would be cured by a touch from their king.*

Monarch and Parliament

As we have seen, the kings and queens of the seventeenth century were much more powerful than they are today. James I and Charles I believed that their power had been given to them by God. Even in Queen Anne's reign people believed that if the queen touched them, they could be cured of certain diseases. Pepys saw Charles II touching the sick to heal them.

Anyone who wanted to get on, came to the royal court. Here they tried to catch the king's attention, or that of a powerful favourite. Each important courtier had a following, called a faction. The factions constantly struggled against each other.

The Stuarts had one serious problem: they were always short of money. Charles II once had to borrow £300 from Pepys. Kings were expected to live off their own money. If they needed extra income through taxes, they had to ask Parliament for it. Because of this Parliament became more powerful. By William's reign most of the government's money came from taxes, as it does today. William and Mary were given their own money separately.

No women could vote in elections for Parliament, and only some men were allowed to do so. It was easy to bribe voters, so election day was like a huge party. Each county was governed by its important families. They looked after law and order. They supervised the collection of taxes, and they were elected to Parliament. In the seventeenth century each county was like a little country.

Left *This engraving of 1640 shows the House of Commons at work, as well as the plans of some of the towns that were represented in Parliament.*

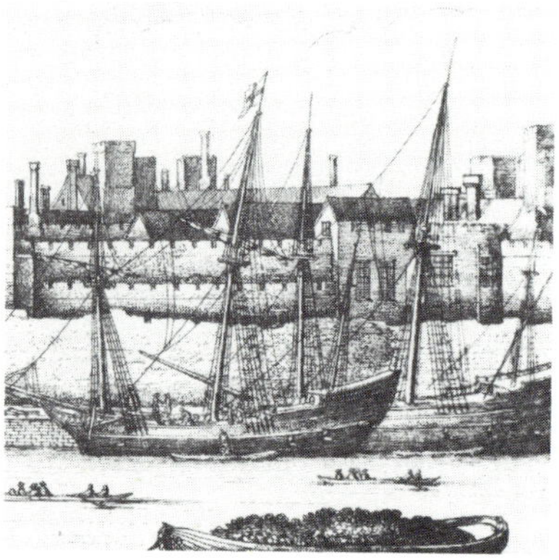

Above *Ships unload their cargoes in London's docks.*

Industry and trade

In the seventeenth century eighty per cent of English people lived in the country. Their chief work was farming. There was very little industry, and there were certainly no factories or industrial towns. The roads were awful — some pot-holes were so big that it was said a man could drown in them. All heavy goods went by boat.

The only really large industry was wool. For centuries the English had been famous for their woollen cloth. In some parts of the country, villages had been pulled down to make way for sheep pasture. Cloth was made in the homes of ordinary people who lived in the country, then gathered together for export.

The coal mining industry was growing rapidly. Most coal came from Newcastle, and was brought down to London by sea. The building trade also flourished, especially in London. 13,200 houses were destroyed in the Great Fire of 1666; they all had to be rebuilt.

Under the Stuarts the English first began to build an empire overseas. By 1713 they had many colonies in North America. In 1664 they drove the Dutch out of a city called New Amsterdam, renaming it New York.

English sailors also set up trading posts in the West Indies and the Far East. They brought many goods in Europe in large quantities for the first time. The most popular were tea, cocoa, coffee and tobacco. By the time of Anne's death the English were one of Europe's leading trading nations. Because of this, Pepys's job of making sure that the navy was in good condition was essential.

Below *Roads were often in an appalling condition and stagecoaches easily became bogged down. The poor state of the transport system slowed down the growth of industry.*

Anglicans and Puritans

Religion was tremendously important in Stuart times. Everyone was expected to go to church on Sunday, couples could be married only in church, and the Church of England controlled schools and universities. Magic was mixed with people's beliefs, too. Several women were killed for being witches.

Until the early sixteenth century, all western Europe had been Roman Catholic. Following a religious change called the Reformation, Christians split into two groups, Catholics and Protestants. The English Church, set up in 1559, was Protestant. But it kept some aspects of the Catholic church, such as bishops and special clothes (called vestments) for clergymen.

The very religious Protestants wanted to purify the Church of England of all traces of Catholicism. Thus they

Right *Women suspected of being witches were submerged in rivers. If they floated they were guilty.*

were called Puritans. James I handled them well, but Charles I annoyed them greatly. Many fought against him in the Civil War. After 1649, when the Puritans controlled the country for a while, they carried out the changes they wanted. Even Christmas was abolished.

When Charles II returned in 1660, Parliament once again made life very difficult for the Puritans. They were prevented from holding good jobs, and Puritan clergymen had to leave the Church of England. Pepys was no Puritan, however. He tells us in his diary that he often went to sleep in church.

Finally, in 1689, the Toleration Act was passed by Parliament. This allowed all Protestants to worship as they wished. Englishmen slowly learned to accept each other's beliefs. The struggle for freedom of worship had been a long and bitter one, and even after 1689 Roman Catholics were not tolerated willingly.

Above *In 1710 angry mobs went on the rampage in London in support of Henry Sacheverell, who had preached against people who were not part of the Church of England.*

Above *William Laud, Archbishop of Canterbury from 1633-40, was suspected of introducing Catholic reforms into the Church of England. This action was one of the causes of the Civil War.*

Roman Catholics

During the Stuart Age most Englishmen saw Catholicism as the religion of their enemies. During the reign of Queen Elizabeth I (1558-1603), Protestant sailors had often fought against the Catholic Spanish. No one would ever forget the defeat of the Spanish Armada in 1588.

At first James I was prepared to help the Catholics. Then something happened which fixed in people's minds the view that Catholics were traitors.

In 1605 a group of important Catholics planned to blow up the king and the Houses of Parliament. They hired cellars under Parliament, and Guy Fawkes filled the cellars with gunpowder. By November the explosives were in place. Then, just in time, the plot was discovered. To this day, each year on 5 November the English celebrate the lucky escape of the king.

For the rest of the seventeenth century the English were terrified of Catholics. When Archbishop Laud tried to alter some customs of the Church of England, he was accused of trying to make England Catholic. Men fought to stop him. Many were suspicious of Charles I, because his wife — Henrietta Maria — was a Catholic. Even at the

Below *The leading conspirators in the Gunpowder Plot of 1605 hoped that by blowing up James I in Parliament, English Catholics would be able to take over the country.*

end of the Stuart Age, James II was driven off the throne because he tried to help the Catholics. Pepys records in his diary how upset he was when his wife one day announced that she was thinking of becoming a Catholic.

The most tragic hatred of Catholics occurred in Ireland, which belonged to England at this time. The Stuarts treated the Irish Catholics very badly. They also encouraged Protestants to settle in northern Ireland. So the terrible problems that there are in Northern Ireland today started in Stuart times.

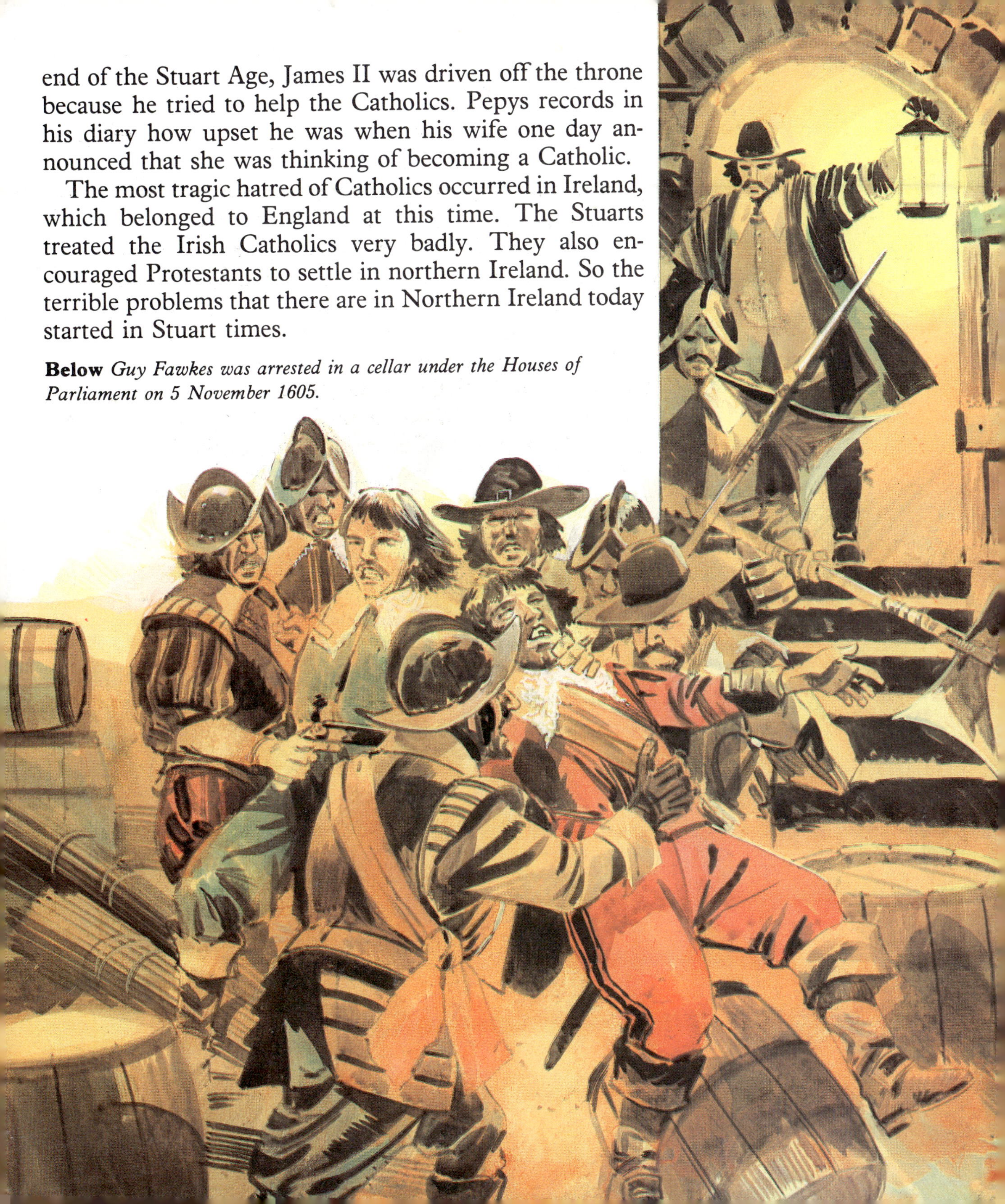

Below *Guy Fawkes was arrested in a cellar under the Houses of Parliament on 5 November 1605.*

4 STUART LONDON

Pepys's city

A German duke visited England at the start of the seventeenth century. He wrote that: 'London is a large, excellent and mighty city of business, and the most important in the whole Kindgom.' In 1603, when the population of England was about 4.7 million, London had 250,000 inhabitants. By 1714, when the population of the whole country was 5.5 million, half a million lived in London.

Below *London Bridge, which spanned the River Thames, supported rows of houses and shops.*

London was really two cities. There was the old City of London, while to the west, joined by the village of Charing Cross, was Westminster. At the heart of London was the River Thames. This great river was a highway, a sewer and a water supply. Three-quarters of England's trade went through London. New docks were being built all the time, such as those at Blackwall in 1614.

A single bridge crossed the Thames. This was London Bridge, a huge structure of twenty arches, with houses and shops on it. In 1617 Fynes Morryson described it as 'among the miracles of the world'. The river rushed so rapidly under the bridge, Pepys said, that going through the arches in a boat was dangerous. For those who did not use the bridge, there were over 2,000 ferries.

The huge city was wealthy — it sided with Parliament during the Civil War and helped it to win. But it was also dirty and dangerous. The narrow streets were crowded with carts, people, horses and rubbish.

Below *A French painting of 1678 shows London from St. Paul's Cathedral on the left to the Tower of London on the right.*

The court and courtiers

Whitehall was the main royal palace during the Stuart Age. The buildings were a rabbit warren of 2,000 rooms, covering 23 acres of Westminster. The men who ran the household were the Lord Chamberlain, the Lord Steward and the Master of the Horse. They employed thousands of servants, from cooks to gardeners.

During the day hundreds of visitors tried to get into the palace. The lucky ones might catch a glimpse of the monarch dining in public at midday. However, many of the Stuarts did not like Whitehall. They found it too large, old-fashioned and cold. James I went away hunting a great deal. Anne preferred living in St. James's Palace.

The kings and queens ran their court in different ways. James I's was extravagant, with many plays and much

Above *Charles II's court was a lively place, full of music, dancing and gambling.*

feasting. The court of Charles II was even more lively. Pepys wrote that he heard a courtier say that it was a terrible place for 'gambling, swearing and drinking'. Anne's court, on the other hand, was more dignified. She enjoyed playing cards more than attending banquets.

Whatever the court was like, the great families were expected to be there. It has been estimated that in 1696 there were 160 lords, who had incomes of more than £2,800 a year. Very wealthy men, like the Earl of Newcastle, had incomes of more than £20,000. These men were like little kings.

The great aristocrats had huge estates and at least one large country mansion. They collected works of art, hunted, and travelled about the country. Wherever they went, they spent vast sums of money. The Earl of Bedford spent £1,500 on clothes for himself and his followers for the coronation of Charles II.

Taverns and coffee-houses

Above *Pepys and his friends spent much of their time eating and drinking in taverns like this one.*

On 2 December 1660 Pepys wrote in his diary: 'We went to the Sun tavern, on Fish Street hill. Captain Teddiman gave us dinner. We had very fine food, good music, a great deal of wine. I was very merry . . . My head ached all night.'

This was a typical evening at a tavern in Stuart London where people like Pepys would often hire a private room and have a meal. But when Pepys had work to do, he usually went to a coffee-house.

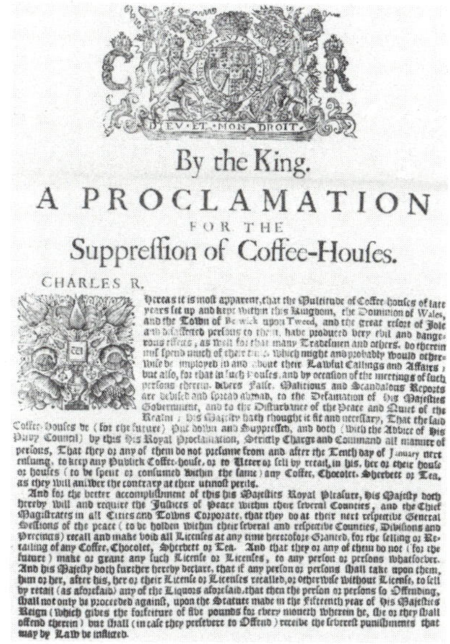

C R

DIEU ET MON DROIT

By the King.

A PROCLAMATION

FOR THE

Suppreſſion of Coffee-Houſes.

CHARLES R.

Whereas it is most apparent, that the Multitude of Coffee-houses of late years set up and kept within this Kingdom, the Dominion of Wales, and the Town of Berwick upon Tweed, and the great resort of Idle and disaffected persons to them, have produced very evil and dangerous effects; as well for that many Tradesmen and others, do therein mis-spend much of their time, which might and probably would otherwise be imployed in and about their Lawful Callings and Affairs; but also, for that in such Houses, and by occasion of the meetings of such persons therein, divers False, Malitious and Scandalous Reports are devised and spread abroad, to the Defamation of His Majesties Government, and to the Disturbance of the Peace and Quiet of the Realm; His Majesty hath thought it fit and necessary, That the said Coffee-houses be (for the future) Put down and Suppressed, and doth (with the Advice of His Privy Council) by this His Royal Proclamation, Strictly Charge and Command all manner of persons, That they or any of them do not presume from and after the Tenth day of January next ensuing, to keep any Publick Coffee-house, or to Utter or sell by retail, in his, her or their house or houses (to be spent or consumed within the same) any Coffee, Chocolet, Sherbett or Tea, as they will answer the contrary at their utmost perils.

And for the better accomplishment of this his Majesties Royal Pleasure, His Majesty doth hereby will and require the Justices of Peace within their several Counties, and the Chief Magistrates in all Cities and Towns Corporate, that they do at their next respective General Sessions of the peace (to be holden within their several and respective Counties, Divisions and Precincts) recall and make void all Licenses at any time heretofore Granted, for the selling or Retailing of any Coffee, Chocolet, Sherbett or Tea. And that they or any of them do not (for the future) make or grant any such License or Licenses, to any person or persons whatsoever. And his Majesty doth further hereby declare, that if any person or persons shall take upon them, him or her, after his, her or their License or Licenses recalled, or otherwise without License, to sell by retail (as aforesaid) any of the Liquors aforesaid, that then the person or persons so Offending, shall not only be proceeded against, upon the Statute made in the Fifteenth year of His Majesties Reign (which gives the forfeiture of five pounds for every moneth wherein he, she or they shall offend therein) but shall (in case they persevere to Offend) receive the severest punishments that may by Law be inflicted.

Above *In 1675 Charles II closed all coffee-houses because they were places where politics were freely discussed and he suspected that this would encourage opposition to his government.*

The first coffee-house opened in Oxford in 1650. By 1686, Edward Lloyd's coffee house in Tower Street had become the place where insurance dealers met. Today Lloyd's is still the name of London's famous insurance business.

Coffee houses (or chocolate-houses) were the meeting places for rich and poor, businessmen, writers and politicians. There men and women discussed the latest news and ideas. The government didn't like talk of politics, and in 1675 they ordered coffee-houses to be closed. No one took any notice. Later the political parties used coffee-houses as their headquarters: the Whigs met in Kid's, the Tories in Jonathan's.

Behaviour in the coffee-houses was usually quite good. The taverns, on the other hand, were rough. At that time most men carried weapons, and fights frequently broke out. There were no street lights in Stuart London. Men returning home from a tavern always ran the risk of being attacked by gangs of robbers who roamed the dark lanes.

Above *Rats — the carriers of plague — were so common in London that rat-catchers were employed to kill them.*

Above *The streets of London rang with the cries of people selling their goods. This man sold glass tubes of varying lengths.*

In the backstreets

London was a rough city. A few of the buildings were large, and built of brick or stone. Some of the streets were wide. But most houses were cramped and wooden, and most streets were narrow. They were either cobbled or just mud tracks. Several lanes, such as Fleet Street, had open streams flowing down the middle of them. These were filled with dirt and sewage. In the summer the smell was horrible.

The city was tremendously crowded. Poor people came from the country, seeking their fortune. The rich came to try their luck at court. Merchants lived in London because of its commercial importance. Just as today, many Englishmen and women visited London to see the sights.

Because London was so big, thieves, thugs, highwaymen, cheats and other bad characters were difficult to catch. Villains escaped to London. Here they could remain in hiding, in a tavern or similar shady place. Many poor citizens were driven to crime when times were hard.

Housing for poor people was densely-packed and dangerous. A family often shared one room, with no water or lavatory. There were no building regulations, so houses were badly built and sometimes collapsed, burying those in them. Buildings jutted out above the ground floor. In some places it was possible to cross a street between two upper-storey windows.

Those who lived in the backstreets of the city feared two things above all else: plague and fire. During Pepys's life London faced both these perils within the space of two years.

Opposite *There was much crime in Stuart London. This pickpocket is escaping from his pursuers over the rooftops.*

Above *In 1666, Londoners fled in panic as the Great Fire of London burned out of control, destroying large areas of the city.*

Plague and fire

'This month ends with great sadness everywhere because of the size of the plague . . . Every day we receive sadder and sadder news of its spread. 6,102 people died of the plague in London this week.' Pepys wrote this on 31 August 1665.

In Stuart times medicine was not well understood. People did not wash much, so they had fleas. They did not realize that these fleas carried a deadly disease, which we now call bubonic plague. In 1665, 68,000 died of it in London. The poor, who lived in dirty slums, were worst hit. Every morning men passed through the streets with

carts, calling 'Bring out your dead'.

Just as the city was recovering from the disaster of the plague, another tragedy struck. On 2 September 1666 a fire broke out in a baker's shop in Pudding Lane. The weather was dry and a breeze was blowing. That night 360 houses were burned down. The fire grew stronger and stronger. Pepys wrote: 'We saw the fire like an arch . . . I wept when I saw it. Churches and houses were all flaming at once. The noise of the flames and the cracking houses was horrid.'

The fire raged for four days and nights. Finally it was extinguished, but not before 400 streets had been destroyed. Luckily not many people were hurt, and the city was soon re-built. The new streets were wider and many fine buildings were constructed. The most famous was St. Paul's Cathedral.

Above *In the cramped insanitary conditions of London, thousands died during the Great Plague of 1665.*

Above *Jonathan Swift (1667-1745), journalist and author of* Gulliver's Travels.

Arts and architecture

Pepys often went to the theatre. Indeed, more good plays were written in the Stuart Age than in any other century. William Shakespeare, the most famous playwright of all, wrote many of his plays during the reign of James I. In his play *Macbeth*, which was set in Scotland, Shakespeare was complimentary about James. Pepys was less complimentary about Shakespeare. He described *A Midsummer Night's Dream* (one of Shakespeare's finest plays) as 'the most weak, ridiculous play that I ever saw in my life'.

Many beautiful poems were also written in the Stuart Age. James I appointed the first poet laureate, Ben Jonson; but probably the best poetry was written by the Puritan, John Milton. Writers made money by working for the political parties. Jonathan Swift, who later wrote *Gulliver's Travels*, wrote pamphlets attacking the Whigs. Newspapers appeared for the first time in the late seventeenth century. Swift wrote for a Tory one, called the *Examiner*.

In 1615 James I employed an architect called Inigo Jones to design the rebuilding, or improvements to royal

houses. He believed that the most attractive style of architecture was that of the Ancient Greeks and Romans, so he introduced it to England. The buildings he designed stand out against the traditional architecture of his time.

After the Great Fire of London four-fifths of the city had to be rebuilt. Christopher Wren drew up a plan for the rebuilding only a few days after the fire had been put out. His plan was not followed, but he did design forty-nine churches as well as St. Paul's Cathedral.

Above *Sir Christopher Wren (1632-1723), architect of St. Paul's Cathedral.*

Below *in a scene from* Gulliver's Travels, *Gulliver is held captive by the tiny people of Lilliput.*

5 COUNTRY TOWNS

Bristol — a thriving port

Above *The City Arms of Bristol.*
Below *A woodcut of Puritans heading towards a port to sail to America to escape religious persecution.*

In 1668 Samuel and Elizabeth Pepys went on a holiday. They travelled west to Oxford, Salisbury and Bath, before arriving in Bristol on the afternoon of the 13 June. Pepys was impressed by the city. He called it 'a large and noble place . . . in every way like another London.'

Bristol was an important city. It was the second biggest port in the country, and by 1700 it had a population of 20,000. It was 'a city of great trade'. Each year 240 ships used its docks. They carried cloth and English manufactures to all corners of the world. In return they brought

back sugar, wine, tobacco and cotton.

From Bristol, settlers sailed to newly-discovered countries. On 10 April 1625 two ships set sail for Virginia. They carried forty-three people, and all the goods they would need to set up a colony in the 'New World': canvas, needles, pickaxes, saws and other useful tools. So the early Americans left from Bristol.

Through its trade, Bristol had become a wealthy city. Its famous families, such as the Colstons, were among the best-known in the land. There were grand churches and smart houses. There was even Bristol milk, a special Spanish wine which was given to visitors.

The only complaint that tourists made of Bristol was that it was too crowded. The author, Daniel Defoe, went there in Anne's reign. He said that there wasn't room for one more house in the whole city.

Above *Ships crewed by Puritans leave Bristol on the start of a voyage to America to set up a colony.*

Oxford — a royal town

Pepys called Oxford 'a very sweet place'. It was smaller than Bristol, with about 5,000 inhabitants in the reign of James I. It had little industry, but ran a large market. The most important part of the city was its university.

The Stuarts were fond of Oxford. When an outbreak of plague made London too dangerous to live in, the court sometimes moved to Oxford. Three times Stuart kings called parliaments to meet there. The last time this happened, in 1681, Charles II was trying to defeat the Whigs. He knew that Whig MPs — less royalist than the Tories — would feel uncomfortable in Oxford because it had been the headquarters of Charles I during the years of

the Civil War.

In 1622 Oxford had eighteen colleges and about 2,500 students. Some students were there to work seriously. Others went because their fathers told them to. There were fights between the students and the townspeople these were known as 'town versus gown'. No women were allowed to work at the university and the teachers were not allowed to marry.

Like Pepys, Daniel Defoe was also very impressed by Oxford. He loved the old stone colleges and their quiet atmosphere. The city had everything, he wrote, 'to make the life of the scholars easy and comfortable'. It did not have the bustle of Bristol, or the size of London. But of all the Stuart towns, Oxford must have been one of the most pleasant to live in. It was never as badly affected by the plague as other towns.

Opposite *Fights between 'town and gown' (townspeople and students) in Oxford could be violent.*
Below *University College, Oxford, as it looked in 1675.*

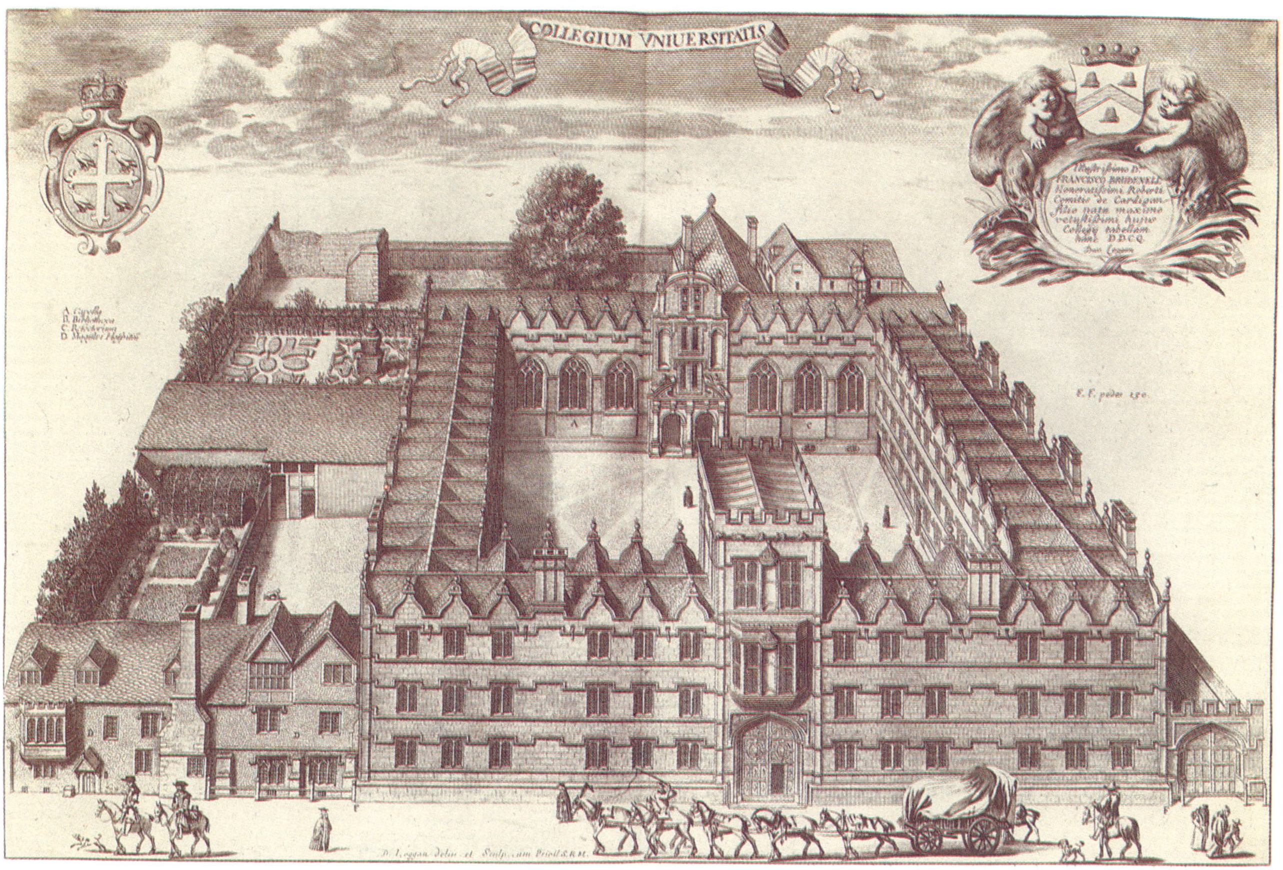

6 COUNTRY LIFE

Above *A typical summer scene in the countryside, where most people lived and worked.*

On the farm

Most English families lived very differently from those of Pepys and the Stuart monarchs. They dwelt in the countryside, in small damp houses. They worked hard, and usually died young. For these ordinary people, if the harvest was poor, famine was never very far away.

In many parts of the country, especially in the Midlands, farmers worked on huge open fields. A village had three or four fields round it, and a family had several strips of land in each field. Villagers shared ploughs, and their pigs and cattle grazed on common land. Farming methods had not changed for hundreds of years.

Kent was a region that was farmed differently. Here there were private farms, as we have today. Some were small, and worked by one family; others were huge estates, which employed many labourers.

Finally, there were large areas of grazing land in East Anglia, Yorkshire and the South West. Here thousands of sheep produced the wool that made the merchants rich. However, not many of the farmers and shepherds who worked for wages became rich. Their pay was 10d (4p) for a day's work.

Apart from the plough, there was almost no machinery on the farm. Everything, from sowing to harvesting, was done by hand. Few cattle could be kept alive over the long winter months when the grass did not grow, so most of them were slaughtered in the autumn. The meat was salted and smoked to preserve it for the dark days that lay ahead.

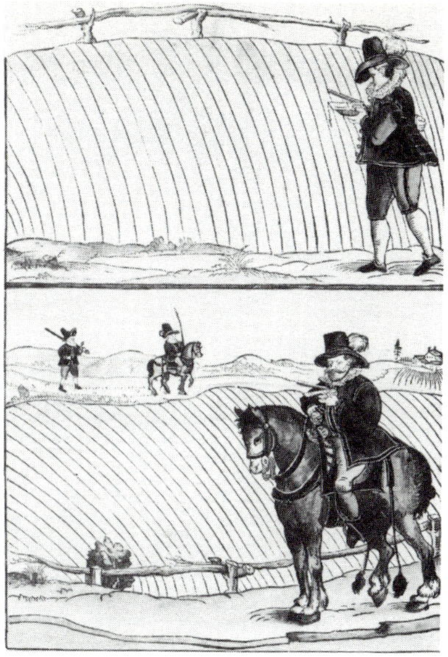

Above *A wealthy farmer surveys his land.*

Above *Many villages had tread wheels, like this one from Catherington in Hampshire. It was operated by a single person who walked on the inside of the wheel, making it turn. The rotating wheel then turned a shaft which lifted the water from the well.*

In the village

At the centre of every village was the church. The lord, or squire, had the largest and smartest house, and the villagers had to take notice of what he said. He was the wealthiest man in the area, and, as a magistrate, was responsible for keeping law and order. Pepys was made a magistrate in 1660, although he said he did not have any idea what he had to do.

The cottages of the villagers in Stuart times were primitive. They were normally thatched and built with wooden frames. The better ones had chimneys and glass in the windows; most were smoky and drafty. Farm labourers had little furniture. Perhaps a table, some chairs and a bed were all they possessed.

Country people lived their lives according to the season. In the summer they rose with the sun at about 5 a.m. — even Pepys frequently got up at this time. For breakfast the farm labourer had ale and bread. Cheese, bread and ale were probably all he had to eat at midday and in the evening. Only half the population could afford meat every day of the week.

Most Englishmen drank a good deal. The rich, of which Pepys was one, drank wine; the poor drank ale. This was one of the few pleasures that the ordinary man enjoyed, and every village had several taverns.

You can see the clothes that the villagers wore in the picture. The women wore long gowns and petticoats. Men were dressed in leather or woollen trousers (called breeches), shirts and jackets. Both men and women usually wore hats.

Opposite *Villagers gather around to listen to a travelling preacher. As you can see some people listened carefully, but others laughed at what the preacher had to say.*

Sports and pastimes

For those who could afford it, the most popular sport in Stuart times was hunting. In the summer James I went deer hunting almost every day. Charles II, as Pepys tells us, also enjoyed 'hunting of a stag', but he took pleasure in yachting and horse racing too.

The village green was the place where ordinary people relaxed. In the summer they danced round maypoles, played bowls and enjoyed fairs. The game of cricket was just starting. Football was a rough game played more like

Below *Football was a violent, but popular, sport played with very few rules between big teams.*

modern rugby, with huge teams and very few rules.

Some Stuart entertainments were very cruel. Bears were chained to poles and tormented by dogs until they died. Cocks were set fighting with sharp spurs on their legs. Large sums of money were bet on cockfights, and one of the wretched birds was nearly always killed.

Quieter people preferred fishing. For the poor, this was a way of getting food; others enjoyed it, as they do today, for its peaceful pleasure. As guns became more accurate, so shooting became more popular. Early in Stuart times the bow and arrow was still widely used.

Indoors, people played cards, or danced formal dances. Pepys spent much of his spare time in taverns, and many people did the same. There was no television or radio. Most people lived miles from a theatre. Even reading was difficult because books were expensive, and at night there was only candle-light to read by.

Above *The design for a playing card in 1710.*

Crime and punishment

Above *In 1660 those responsible for the killing of Charles I were executed.*

'I went to Charing Cross to see Major-General Harrison hanged, drawn and quartered. He looked as cheerful as a person could do in his state. Soon he was cut down off the gallows, and his head and heart were shown to the crowd. There were shouts of joy.' (13 October 1660). Pepys did not think that what was done to Harrison was cruel. Justice in Stuart England was merciless.

Because there were so many poor people, there was more crime in Pepys's time than there is today. Most men carried swords, and arguments easily turned into dangerous fights. Thousands of men and women could live only if they stole enough money to live on. Highwaymen and robbers terrified travellers, and towns were full of pickpockets. In hard times there were serious

riots in many parts of the country.

The law was not very just. Until the end of the century, the king could dismiss judges if he didn't like what they did. Magistrates were harsh on criminals, and juries were often bullied by rude judges.

There was no police force in the seventeenth century, but when criminals were caught, they were punished fiercely. Until 1642 torture was allowed when questioning suspicious people. Thieves were hung, tramps were branded and whipped. People who went bankrupt were sent to prison until they paid their debts. They could not earn money in prison, so they usually stayed there until they died.

For lesser crimes a victim was sent to the pillory. He had to stand in a public place with his head and hands locked in a wooden board. Passers-by hurled insults or rotten vegetables at the criminal's head.

Above *Highwaymen often robbed carriages as they travelled along dark and lonely roads.*

7 THE STUART AGE

Samuel Pepys lived at a time of much change. During the seventeenth century England built up an overseas empire. By 1714 she had a whole string of colonies on the east coast of North America. These colonies later became the English-speaking United States of America. Other colonies and trading posts were set up in the West Indies (Jamaica and Barbados for example), and at Madras and Calcutta in India.

Pepys also lived in an age of great scientific change. Stuart scientists made important discoveries. For example, William Harvey discovered the circulation of the blood, and Sir Isaac Newton explained gravity for the first time. Charles II personally helped the development of science. He joined a group of scientists who met to discuss their work; from 1661 they were known as the Royal Society. Pepys joined in 1665. From 1684-86 he had the honour of being the Society's President, 'a most acceptable thing'.

The Stuart Age in many ways marked the beginning of the world as we know it today. Religious toleration started with the Toleration Act of 1689 and modern government, science, and the arts all have their roots in the seventeenth century. We are particularly lucky, therefore, that we have the diaries of Samuel Pepys to show us so clearly what life was like in those exciting times.

Opposite *The illustration shows general scenes of the British army advancing at the battle of Blenheim, St. Paul's Cathedral on fire, settlers trading with Indians and a warship firing its guns.*
Left *A portrait of Sir Isaac Newton.*

Table of dates

1566 Birth of James Stuart, later James I of England.
1603 James I comes to the throne.
1605 Gunpowder plot.
1625 James I dies, Charles I becomes king.
1628 Duke of Buckingham assassinated. William Harvey discovers the circulation of blood.
1629 Charles I decides to rule without Parliament.
1633 Samuel Pepys born.
1638 Scots rebel against the English.
1640 Parliament meets for the first time for eleven years.
1642 Civil War breaks out.
1645 Charles I defeated at the battle of Naseby.
1646-50 Pepys at St. Paul's School.
1648 Royalists defeated by Oliver Cromwell.
1649 Charles I beheaded.
1651-4 Pepys studies at Magdalen College, Cambridge.
1654 Pepys becomes Secretary to Sir Edward Montague.
1655 Pepys marries Elizabeth St. Michael.
1658 Oliver Cromwell dies.
1660 Charles II returns to England. Pepys starts his diary and is appointed clerk to the Navy Board.
1665 War against the Dutch. Great Plague in London.
1666 Great Fire of London.
1669 Elizabeth Pepys dies. Pepys stops writing his diary.
1673 Pepys becomes Secretary to the Admiralty and a Member of Parliament.
1679 Pepys is imprisoned in the Tower of London for a few weeks.
1685 Death of Charles II, James II becomes king. Battle of Sedgemoor. Duke of Monmouth defeated.
1687 Publication of *In Principia,* Sir Isaac Newton's great work about gravity.
1688 James II flees to France, William III and Mary II become king and queen.
1689 Passing of the Toleration Act and the Bill of Rights.
1694 Queen Mary dies.
1702 Death of William III, Anne becomes queen.
1703 Samuel Pepys dies.
1704 John Churchill, the Duke of Marlborough, defeats the French at the battle of Blenheim.
1707 Act of Union between England and Scotland.
1714 Death of Queen Anne, the last of the Stuarts.
1825 Samuel Pepys's diaries published.

Glossary

Admiralty The government department which runs the navy.

Architect A person who designs buildings.

Aristocrat Someone of noble birth.

Assassinate To kill an important person, usually for political reasons.

Bankrupt A person who fails in business through lack of money.

Branded Burned with a hot iron to make a mark on the skin.

Catholic (or Roman Catholic) A member of the Christian Church of which the pope is head.

Civil Servant Someone who works for the government.

Civil War A war fought between two sides from the same country.

Cobble A rounded stone used in paving.

Colony A country, taken over by settlers from another nation, which remains a subject of that ruling nation.

Dock Part of a harbour where ships load and unload.

Drawn and quartered Cut into pieces.

Election A time when people vote to decide who goes to Parliament.

Empire Many lands ruled by one powerful country.

Export To send goods out of a country.

Extravagant Spending a great deal of money.

Famine Widespread hunger and starvation.

Fleas Small insects that live on animals and humans.

Gallows A wooden framework for hanging criminals.

Magistrate An important gentleman who sees that the law is obeyed in his neighbourhood.

Mansion A large house.

Monarch A king or queen.

'New World' North, Central and South America, so called because the area was unknown to Europeans until the end of the fifteenth century.

Plague A widespread outbreak of disease.

Poet laureate The poet chosen by the monarch to write especially for the court.

Prosperity Wealth.

Protestants Christians who broke away from the Roman Catholic Church in the sixteenth century.

Revolution Complete change.

Roundheads Supporters of Parliament in the English Civil War. Supporters of the king were called Cavaliers, or Royalists.

Squire A country gentleman.

Stag A male deer.

Tavern A public house ('pub').

Tax Money paid to the government.

Traitor Someone who betrays his country.

Tyrant Someone who uses power harshly or cruelly.

Further information

Places to visit

Museums Every county in Britain — and many states in eastern America whose early history is linked to those people who sailed there from Stuart England — has a museum open to the public. It is a good idea to investigate your nearest museum to see if they exhibit any artefacts or paintings from the Stuart period. To find out about Pepys's navy, visit the National Maritime Museum at Greenwich, built by Sir Christopher Wren. Also try to visit the Museum of London to see their exhibition about the Great Fire of London.

Famous sites There are a large number of Stuart buildings still standing in Britain today. The most famous is St. Paul's Cathedral, designed by Wren and built from 1675-1710. Downing Street dates from Stuart times. So does Kensington Palace and the Banqueting House at Whitehall, designed by Inigo Jones in 1622. All are worth a visit. The first American universities date from the seventeenth century. Harvard University was founded in 1640, shortly after the death of its benefactor, John Harvard, a Puritan minister who emigrated from England.

Libraries The local library can always give information about the best places to visit both near your home and further afield. Most libraries have a section on local history. Try and find out what was going on in your area during Stuart times.

Books

Ashley, M., *Life in Stuart England* (Batsford)

Barbary, James, *Puritan and Cavalier — the English Civil War* (Gollancz 1978)

Cowie, L.W., *The Trial and Execution of Charles I* (Wayland 1972) and *Plague and Fire, London 1665-66* (Wayland 1972)

Jones, Madeline, *Growing up in Stuart Times* (Batsford) and *Stuart People* (Batsford 1978)

Peoples of the Past series, *Everyday Life in the Seventeenth Century* (Macdonald Educational 1983)

Pepys, Samuel, *The Diaries of Samuel Pepys,* ed. by Robert Latham and William Matthews, (Bell and Hyman 1978)

Routh, C.R.N. (Ed.) *They saw it happen: 1485-1688* (Basil Blackwell 1956)

Unstead, R.J., *Tudors and Stuarts* (A&C Black) and *Living in Samuel Pepys's London* (A&C Black 1975)

White-Thomson, S.J., *Oliver Cromwell and the Civil War* (Wayland 1984)

Wodzicka, Helen, *The Glorious Age of Charles II* (Wayland 1973)

Index

America 42, 43, 55
Anglicans (Church of England) 26, 27, 28
Anne 20, 22, 43, 55
  character 20
  court 20, 33
  French war 20
  political parties 20
Architecture 40, 41

Blenheim, battle of 20, 55
Bristol 42, 43, 44, 45
Buckingham, Duke of 12
Building 24

Cards 33, 51
Catholics 11, 15, 16, 26, 27, 28, 29
Charles I 6, 22, 52
  character 12
  and Civil War 13, 44
  execution 6, 7, 13, 14
  and Henrietta Maria 29
  and Parliament 12, 13
  and religion 13, 27, 28
Charles II 8, 16, 22, 33, 35, 50, 55
  character 14
  court 14, 33, 44
  in exile 7, 14, 32
  restoration 4, 7, 14, 15, 27
  and succession crisis 15
Churchill, John, Duke of Marlborough 26
Churchill, Sarah 20
Civil War, the English 6, 7, 13, 27, 28, 31, 44
Clothes 48
Coal 24
Coffee-houses 34, 35
Colonies 24, 43, 55
Court (see individual Kings and Queens)
Crime 35, 36, 52, 53
Cromwell, Oliver 7, 14

Defoe, Daniel 43, 45
Diet 48

Education 45
Elections 22, 23
Elizabeth I 15, 28

Farming 24, 46, 47
Fawkes, Guy 28, 29
Fire of London 8, 24, 38, 39, 41, 55
Football 50, 51
France 14, 16, 19, 20

George I 20
Godolphin, Sidney 20
Gunpowder Plot 28

Harvey, William 55
Highwaymen 52, 53
Housing 48
Hunting 50

India 55
Industry 24
Ireland 19, 29

Jacobites 19
James I 10, 11, 22, 23, 32, 40, 50, 55
  character 10
  and Catholics 28
  at court 11, 32
  and Parliament 28
  and Puritans 27
  at war 11
James II 9, 16, 18, 19, 20
  character 16
  and Monmouth's rebellion 16
  as Prince of Wales 15
  and religion 16, 29
Jones, Inigo 40, 41
Jonson, Ben 40

Laud, Archbishop 14, 28
London 4, 15, 24, 30, 31, 34, 35, 36, 38, 39, 44, 45
Louis XIV 15, 20

Malplaquet, battle of 20
Mary II 16, 18, 19, 23
Milton, John 40

Naseby, battle of 13
Newcastle 24
Newspapers 40
Newton, Sir Isaac 55

Oudenarde, battle of 20
Oxford 35, 42, 44, 45

Parliament 22, 23, 27, 29, 31 (see Kings & Queens)
Pepys, Elizabeth 7, 9, 42
Pepys, Samuel 10, 14, 22, 23, 27, 29, 31, 33, 34, 36, 38, 39, 40, 42, 44, 45, 48, 50, 51, 52, 55
  as diarist 4, 7, 8, 9
  early life 4, 6
  imprisonment 9
  marriage 7
  and the navy 4, 8, 9, 16, 25
Plague 8, 38, 36, 39, 44, 45
Political parties
  Tories 20, 35, 40, 44
  Whigs 20, 35, 40

Ramillies, battle of 20
Rights, Bill of 19
Roads 24, 25
Roundheads 7

Science 55
Scotland 10, 13, 19, 40
Scott, James, Duke of
Monmouth 16
Sedgemoor, battle of 16
Shakespeare, William 40
Spain 11, 20
St. Paul's Cathedral 39, 41, 55
Swift, Jonathan 40

Taverns 34, 35
Thames, River 16, 30, 31, 51
Theatre 40, 51
Toleration Act 27, 55
Tories (see under
political parties)
Trade 24, 25, 42, 43, 55

Union, Act of 20

Whigs (see political parties)
Whitehall 7, 32
William III 16, 18, 19
war with France 19
and Jacobites 19
and Parliament 18, 19, 23
Witchcraft 26
Wool 24, 27
Wren, Christopher 41

Picture acknowledgements

The illustrations in this book were supplied by: Mansell Collection 45, 54; Weald and Downland Open Air Museum, Singleton, W. Sussex 48; the remainder are from the Wayland Picture Library.